Undercover Bishop

A Parable for the Modern Church

Undercover Bishop: A Parable for the Modern Church
Judith I. Gotwald
creation@dca.net

HOW TO USE THIS BOOK

Undercover Bishop is the tale of three small churches and their relationship with the greater church. The story is presented to promote discussion about issues common to small parishes in many mainline denominations.

The saga can be read as one book for a single broad discussion or broken into segments. If this is the case, the discussion might revolve around each of the three congregations:

- Pleasantville, a small town church;
- Zion, an urban neighborhood church, and
- Grace, a country church on the fringe of encroaching suburbia.

Starter questions are found at the end of the book.

We hope Undercover Bishop helps your congregation or group explore issues facing the modern church. It is often easier to see ourselves in a story than in a mirror—as Jesus knew very well!

Undercover Bishop is fiction, but like all fiction it is drawn from reality. The idea was sparked by the Ambassador visits of Redeemer Lutheran Church, a congregation locked out of the Evangelical Lutheran Church in America in a property dispute with the bishop of the Southeastern Pennsylvania Synod (SEPA).

The concept grew from the popular television show, *Undercover Boss*, where a corporate CEO visits the company workforce incognito to learn about the everyday challenges that contribute to a company's success. Each week, corporate executives visit their own branch offices, thinking they know everything there is to know about their businesses. Invariably, they discover that employees have a different view entirely, even as they display loyalty to their work.

Might the same be true of the Church?

Redeemer Ambassadors spent three years visiting ELCA churches—most, but not all, in SEPA's territory. We visited more than 80 congregations. We participated in worship, observed, and spoke with members and pastors.

Much of the dialog in this parable is drawn from these discussions. Our experience is foundational to this series, but the characters presented are fictional and do not depict any actual parish or individual. They are composites of the many visits we've made and our own experiences. Much of the dialog comes from our visits.

Redeemer's Ambassador visits reveal truths that are difficult for church members and clergy to discern when isolated in their own parishes and clusters or the confines of their job descriptions. We hope Undercover Bishop sheds some light on accepted ministry practices and helps further ministry to the benefit of all.

DEDICATION

This book is dedicated to the memory of loyal Redeemer member Marilyn Popp.

Marilyn was a school teacher and dedicated to the children of the city. She would have been a college student when America's cities were experiencing the unrest of the Civil Rights movement, but she never wavered in her passion to serve the children wherever she was assigned in the City of Philadelphia. She and her husband made their home in one of Philadelphia's poorest neighborhoods, Germantown.

Marilyn attended Jonathan Pritchard Memorial Lutheran Church as a girl. She had no family support in the pursuit of her faith. She attended church with friends.

Marilyn left the Lutheran Church to raise her daughter with her husband in the Roman Catholic Church.

She and her husband had attended a Bach concert at Redeemer in the late 1990s. Her husband died suddenly days later. Heartbroken, Marilyn returned to her Lutheran roots and joined Redeemer. She always sat in the pew she and her husband, Joe, had occupied on their last visit to church together.

She was not named in the synod's lawsuits against individual members of Redeemer, but she attended most of the hearings—long after our pastors disappeared!

About a year after Redeemer congregation was locked out of its sanctuary, Marilyn made a comment. She was hurt, along with the rest of our congregation, and on this Sunday morning she was tired. After our house worship, Marilyn commented. "I just don't understand why they [SEPA Synod] want a church without us in it."

That comment sparked Redeemer's Ambassadors program. We decided to put an end to our imposed isolation and begin visiting the churches who voted to take our property. We wanted to understand why we were so unwelcome in the church many of us had served all our lives. Marilyn accompanied us on almost all of our church visits. She loved worship and church architecture and had already seen her beloved childhood parish close. She longed—as we all do—for the day we might return to our building.

She was one of Redeemer's strongest and most valued leaders.

Our last visit with Marilyn was to Spirit and Truth Lutheran Church in Yardley, Pa, just outside of West Philadelphia. We entered an empty sanctuary that morning, waited for about 20 minutes, and then gave up on worship and went to breakfast together. Over coffee, she commented, "I'm beginning to think I'll never see the inside our our church again." She died three days later.

The Ambassadors continued our visits, but they weren't as enjoyable without our leader.

Well done, faithful servant. Marilyn, may you rest in peace and in the knowledge of the Lord.

1
A New Bishop Takes Office

Ruby Kinisa walked into her new office for the first time since her installation as bishop of the NorthEastWestSouth Synod of the National Lutheran Church (NEWS-NLC). She had been in the office many times in her six years as a synod staff member. As she sank into the plush executive chair, she suddenly felt the weight of responsibility for 200 parishes in the 1500-square-mile regional office.

She swiveled toward the window but turned back to her desk when she heard a soft knock on the open door.

"I see you are settling in, Ruby, or should I address you as Bishop Kinisa now," Gil Ableman ventured with his characteristic grin.

"Come on in, Gil! I'll always be Ruby to you." Bishop Kinisa greeted her colleague of many years with genuine affection.

The two had served together in the NEWS office for the last six years. The Rev. Gilbert Ableman had worked for the synod even longer—as long as Ruby could remember. He had come from a long family tradition of ministry and had served several small parishes. He had taught Ruby the ropes when she first came to the synod office after graduating from seminary at the top of her class and serving five years as an associate pastor of a mid-sized, suburban congregation.

It was hard for anyone to imagine the synod office without Gil Ableman. He was well respected and had been nominated for bishop twice. He had declined consideration, which puzzled many but surprised no one.

Bishop Kinisa saw an envelope in Gil's hand. "Did you bring the parish reports?" she asked.

"Sure did! Spent all weekend putting them in a form that wouldn't take an entire term to read," Gil said as he handed her a large envelope.

"Thanks, Gil. Pull up a chair. Let's take a look together."

Bishop Kinisa opened the envelope and pulled out a spiral bound report. She flipped through the pages.

"Seems a little light. Are all the reports here?"

"All the reports that were submitted." Gil said. "Actually, it's a better showing than most years, but only a few more than half of the churches filed reports this year."

"You're kidding! The pastors know this is part of their job."

"They know, all right. They just lack incentive," Gil said cryptically.

"I'll give them incentive," Bishop Kinisa replied in a huff. "Draft an email. Send it to every active pastor. From now on it's a requirement."

Gil coughed to hide his amusement.

"Did I say something funny?" Bishop Kinisa asked, surprised and a bit annoyed.

"No disrespect intended," Gil apologized. "It's just that you are the fourth bishop I've served as secretary and statistician, and you are the fourth bishop to start a term by trying to rein in the pastors."

"I can't believe that pastors are so irresponsible. What's the matter with them?" Bishop Kinisa said, more exasperated than embarrassed.

"It's been a long time since either of us have been parish pastors," Gil offered diplomatically. "Take a look at the reports and you'll see."

Bishop Kinisa opened the report to the first page.

Gil explained, "The first section includes line graphs. The opening graph combines the statistics for all the reporting parishes. Each congregation has a small, separate graph."

Bishop Kinisa scanned the document.

"Do the graphs represent attendance, membership or giving?" she asked.

"All three — not that it makes much difference." Gil answered. "You'll notice that with very few exceptions all the trends are down."

"I've worked here long enough to know that all mainline churches are in decline," Bishop Kinisa said impatiently. "We talk about it all the time in this office. But I've never seen it presented this way. It's .... "

She paused, searching for the best word.

"Shocking?" Gil offered.

"More than that." Bishop Kinisa said. "It's troubling. If every church is struggling, we face some serious challenges."

"I'm glad you realize that!" Gil said. "Now you know why I didn't want your job."

Ruby began to wonder what she was in for.

"Look toward the back of the document," Gil suggested. "You'll see the list of churches that have no Sunday School or summer educational program. I'll save you the trouble of counting. It's more than half. Many of our churches all but shut down for three months every year."

Bishop Kinisa turned page after page, sighing audibly. "How long has it been like this?" she mused out loud. She wasn't expecting an answer, but Gil responded.

"No one seems to have an answer. Every time I meet with a new bishop, I think things will change, but I have to be honest with you. Bishoping is tough work, Ruby. You are about to be drawn and quartered."

Ruby paused for a moment, but then became a bit defensive. "Look, Gil. I'm no spring chicken. I've been working in the synod office for six years. I know a thing or two."

"Ruby, I mean no offense and I sincerely wish you the best as bishop, but if you think you are in control, you are wrong. There's not much more I can tell you. You'll find out for yourself."

"I've a mind to give you notice right now," she muttered, knowing Gil could bear her anger without feeling attacked. She softened quickly. "I suspect I need you in my corner. I still say we start by insisting pastors file reports. We can't fix problems without accurate information. After all, the pastors work for us."

Gil interjected. "Actually, the pastors work for the congregations, at least in this earthly sphere."

"I know. I know. We're interdependent. That's the Lutheran way. I just can't understand how pastors can show up at the annual assembly without fulfilling their obligations."

Gil attempted an explanation. "It's hard to explain. My guess is that the statistics are so poor that reporting them is inviting criticism. The pastors would rather take the heat for not filing a report than for filing reports that are so dismal."

Bishop Kinisa dropped the report on her desk. "How am I, as bishop, supposed to be able to help congregations if I don't know their problems?"

"That, Ruby, is something we are going to have to figure out—the sooner the better."

Both colleagues sat for a long moment in silence.

Finally, Bishop Kinisa ventured an idea. "I am going to meet with every pastor and get to the bottom of this."

"Sounds good," Gil said. "But you already know all 250 on the roster. Pastors need you on their side. If they want a new call, they will want your support. The pastors are going to tell you what they think you want to hear."

"Then I'll go to the congregations."

"Careful with that. Pastors will feel threatened and congregations are not likely to rock the boat.

Some of them have had some bad experiences with your predecessors. They will talk to you out of respect, but don't expect candor."

"There must be a way," Bishop Kinisa insisted.

"You know as well as I that parish dynamics are tricky."

Another long silence.

"What if the people don't know they are talking to the bishop? How about..." Ruby paused, rounding up the many ideas spinning in her mind. "How about I go into a few congregations undercover?" Bishop Kinisa ventured.

Gil took a moment to ponder the idea. He shook his head. "How are you going to pull that off? Everybody knows you! Besides, nobody likes to be fooled. It could come back to bite you."

"Let's both think about that overnight. Let me get back to work now. Come in tomorrow morning with your best ideas."

2
The Plot Thickens

Gil Ableman arrived at work early the next morning and was surprised to see the door to the office suite unlocked. He found Bishop Ruby Kinisa at the coffee machine in the break room.

"Hi, Gil! Can I pour you a cup?" she asked as she added some powdered creamer to her mug.

"Thanks," Gil replied. "I've never needed a good cup of coffee more."

"Rough night, I'm guessing—if your night was anything like mine," Ruby said.

The two colleagues sat across from each other at the round break table.

"I'm just not sure about this 'Undercover Bishop' idea," Gil confessed. "I foresee a lot of potential problems."

"I have concerns, too. But I'm convinced there may be some good in the idea," the Bishop responded with a touch of enthusiasm. "I'd be a fool if I didn't hear you out, though. We've got a good hour before the staff starts filtering in. Shoot!"

"Well, I'm just a believer in transparency," Gil started, "especially in the Church. We are dealing with people who trust us. We can't risk playing with their faith."

"Good point. But didn't you suggest to me yesterday that people don't trust us. That's the one thing you said yesterday that kept me awake last night. You said some of the churches have had bad experiences with the synod. I must confess, I don't know much about that. Fill me in."

Gil took a few long sips of coffee. "I haven't worked in these offices for more than twenty years by telling stories on former bishops. Let me just say that in a few parishes, some questionable things happened. It's hard to explain—broken promises, conflicting agendas. The bishop at the time just wasn't on the same page with the congregations. The congregations felt betrayed. Their pastors—if they had one—ended up feeling pressured from both the synod and the congregation. Let's just say it hasn't always been pretty."

"Gil, you have to be open with me. I have to know the synod's most vulnerable situations. I must confess, I am stunned at some of what you are telling me. I have the utmost respect for everyone in this office, past and present."

"That wall of respect is part of the problem." Gil said. "No one wants to criticize church leaders, myself included. Uncomfortable problems are often swept under the rug. But here's a clue. I'm talking to you today because I'm tired. I've been watching from the sidelines for 24 years. Now that I'm nearing retirement, I want to see real change."

"Are you saying you feel guilty?"

"I've been trying to avoid that word, but yes." Gil answered sheepishly. "I'm no different than anyone else. I've been protecting my job when I should have been speaking to previous bishops the way I'm speaking to you now. That being said, I can't break old habits overnight."

"I see you have no intention of naming names."

"Oh, I could, but it will be best for you to discover things on your own. I don't want to add to the prejudice. Let's go to your office and take a look at the congregational roster."

Gil took a moment to pour a second cup of coffee before following Ruby to her office.

By the time he joined the new bishop, she had the congregational roster up on her computer screen.

"Pull your chair around so you can see the screen." she invited Gil. "What am I looking for?"

"Find the congregations with the least pastoral help. That's a sure sign of a broken relationship with the synod."

Ruby scanned the list, glossing over the names most familiar to her. "You know, for the last six years I concentrated on my own territory in the synod. I had about 50 parishes, all in the suburbs. But to tell you the truth, fifteen of them took 90% of my time. I've rarely been to the city churches. I'm not even sure where some of these neighborhoods are. I don't know much about the small town or country churches either."

"So tell me, what is your impression of the city and country churches?" Gil ventured.

"Well, I guess from what I've heard that most of them are doomed and just hanging on as long as the money lasts." Bishop Kinisa confessed. "Some say they are a financial burden. Some call them social clubs. I've never paid too much attention to tell you the truth. They weren't my problem!"

"You are proving my point about prejudice," Gil was eager to point out. "That's been the attitude of most clergy for the past twenty years. Most are busy in their own parish and have rarely visited other Lutheran congregations. The pastors really don't know much about them. Somebody says something about a congregation and everybody adopts that view."

Gil continued. His pent up passion was starting to show. "Many of the urban churches and country churches have had no contact with the synod office for years. Some have pastors — most of them parttime. Some share pastors. Some find pastoral help on their own. A number of retired clergy are working with these congregations 'off the grid,' so to speak."

"Would I be correct in guessing they have no money?"

"Yes and no. Some have endowments. Some own substantial property holdings. Some have schools that provide an income. Money is a concern, but they get by."

"Hmm. I'm looking now at benevolence giving. It's almost nonexistent," Bishop Kinisa noticed. "Why should we serve congregations that aren't paying their way?"

Gil cleared his throat. Bishop Kinisa was beginning to read his nonverbal signals.

"I've said something wrong, haven't I?" Ruby asked.

"Let me just say this," Gil answered with difficulty. "It isn't always what it seems in church work. If you are going to serve this synod well, Ruby, you have to find these answers on your own. I can only guide you. It's not that I don't want to be helpful. I've just seen too many bishops rely on third party information when making decisions that impact entire neighborhoods. I don't want to be part of the prejudice and harm that has resulted."

Ruby was a bit troubled by Gil's attitude but she had respect for her mentor. "All right, Gil. Can you at least suggest a place to start, please?"

"Choose a small urban congregation, a small rural congregation and a small town congregation. Do some research online. Make a plan. That should keep you busy for a while."

Gil continued. "But now I have a big question. How are you going to pull this off? You've just been elected. Your photo has been on the news. The synod website opens to your beaming countenance."

"I'm glad you asked. I thought about this all night. No one can know. Not even synod staff. The NEWS rumor mill is pretty effective! That's why I came here early. I am going to gather what I think I'll need from the office. When the staff comes in—and they should be here soon—I'll announce that I'm headed for a training retreat and will be out of the office for a while. I'll introduce you as 'in charge' while I'm gone. I'll be working at home when I'm not working on this project. When I leave here at noon today, I'll head straight for the hair salon. I intend to create a new persona. Stop by my apartment after work. I'll want your input."

That afternoon, Bishop Kinisa transformed her appearance. She had her tight curls straightened, dyed, restyled and extensions added. She got some make-up advice from the beauticians. She stopped at the mall and bought a couple of trendy pantsuits and accessories. At the last minute, she returned to the hair salon and ordered a wig, styled in her usual hairstyle, so that she could return to her usual look if necessary.

Early in the evening, Gil rang her doorbell and the "new" bishop came to the door.

"Wow! I wouldn't know you." Gil exclaimed. "You look like a new woman. But have you considered your bearing?" Gil asked.

"What do you mean?"

"Ruby, you are a head-turner. When you enter a room, everyone notices. Admit it. You enjoy that! You expect to be the center of attention. That's OK for a bishop, but an undercover bishop will have to be a bit of a shrinking violet, don't you think."

"Never thought of that. Let's practice."

Gil and Ruby spent a couple of hours role-playing. Gil posed questions and suggested a "back story" to make her visit believable.

"I think your new persona is going to work well among lay members, but I don't think you'll fool the pastors. You need a sidekick. I think I know the perfect person. He's a second career, fourth-year seminarian at a school 200 miles away. You can get started. Let me contact Bruce James. If he's up for the challenge, I'll ask him to meet with us."

"Sounds like a plan! Just one more thing, Gil."

"What's that?"

"I've chosen a new name. I was going call myself Scarlett — to go with Ruby — but I'm thinking it will remind me to watch my bearing if I go with Violet — Violet Shepherd."

"See you in a few days —Violet," Gil said on his way out the door.

3
Making A Plan

The next day was Friday. Alone in her apartment, Bishop Kinisa—alias Violet Shepherd—sat in her breakfast nook with her laptop and a mug of coffee. She had identified a dozen congregations that fit Gil's suggestions for size and limited professional leadership. Now she began to look for more information than she could find in the parish reports. One by one she typed the names of the congregations into her computer's search engine. All twelve churches showed up in online directories, but only half led to their own website.

"Hmmm," she thought. "I'd better start keeping notes. This could get confusing."

She found a notebook. She copied the name of each congregation, the pastor's name, church address, phone and website. She left ample room for notes. She thought for a moment about asking Gil to look up the pastors' files, but thought better of it. "Gil is big on minimizing prejudice. Best to go with an open mind!" she thought.

She began to visit websites.

The first church she found was an urban congregation in an old working class neighborhood generally considered home to people of low-to moderate-income families and young singles. She noted that the congregation boasted of its historic roots on the front page.

"Zion Lutheran. Founded in 1759."

"I remember the former bishop talking about this congregation," she thought. "He referred to it as an 'old folks home.' He said it was only a matter of a decade before all the members would be dispatched to their eternal reward and the synod could close the church and sell the property."

She clicked on a tab that promised to introduce Zion's leaders. She saw photos of each church council member with a short bio.

"That's great," she thought. "They look like good solid Lutherans. Six women and a couple of men. None of them looks particularly old and a couple look to be quite young! But there is no photo of the pastor." She wrote a few notes.

She started exploring the website clicking on the various menu tabs.

Worship. *Click*. A page opened with photos of worship obviously taken at Christmas time. She noted that worship was at 10 am. Communion was offered on first and third Sundays of the month.

Social Ministry. *Click*. This page contained photos, too. Some showed a small group wielding hammers and saws, helping to build a home with a national service project that provides homes for low-income families. Another photo showed people getting in a van. The caption read they were making a holiday visit to a nearby prison. Another photo showed the sanctuary chancel steps piled high with canned and packaged food for a food pantry.

Women's Group. *Click*. Ruby saw that the congregation's women's group met on Saturdays. Ruby wrote that down.

The bishop's plan was starting to take shape. She'd attend worship first, but she also planned to attend the women's group on Saturday.

She left the site and searched for a country church. She found one on the far border of the synod's territory that looked promising. She'd heard of this congregation from one of its former pastors but had never visited it.

Click. The opening page of the website looked like it had been created in the early days of the internet with no design—just an attempt at a logo with type overlapping awkwardly.

Grace Lutheran Church
Center Township
All welcome.

The site had only two pages—**About Us** and **From Our Pastor.** The **About Us** page listed Sunday worship time and contact information.

On to the next tab. **From Our Pastor.** *Click.* There was a photo of the previous pastor and a long welcome message. She jotted a few notes and impressions and moved on.

Now she was looking for a church in a small town. She clicked on Google Maps in her menu bar and typed in the name of a town in the central area of the synod. The resulting map included the surrounding regions. She located a church from her list in Pleasantville. She noted that the parish had no pastor. This puzzled her because she was familiar with the published "Parishes in Transition" list and couldn't recall seeing Pleasantville as preparing to call a pastor. *Click.* She went to their web page.

Pleasantville Lutheran Church
serving our community since 1835
All welcome.

Bishop Kinisa was surprised to see a colorful, well-designed opening page. The site had five pages: **About Us, Worship, Our Ministry Team, Education** and **News.**

Ruby decided to explore the tab **Education.** *Click.*

Bible Study, Wednesday nights at 7 pm.
At the church. All welcome.
Topic of study: Philippians.

Then she noticed a second Bible study.

Daytime Bible study
Thursday mornings at 10 am.
Carol Martin's home.

"I wonder who Carol is!" Ruby thought.

Ruby clicked on **News.** There she found a long list of weekday activities. She noted a congregational potluck dinner coming up that very night. "I'll see what I have in the pantry and take it from there," she thought.

She dashed off an email to Gil, just to let him know that her undercover mission was about to launch.

For the rest of the day, Bishop Kinisa worked on office work, preparing for meetings that would be upon her in just a few weeks. She checked in with her executive secretary, who did not bother to hide her dissatisfaction with her absence. Ruby did what she could to smooth things over.

Late in the afternoon she got ready for her first undercover foray.

4
Potluck in Pleasantville

Bishop Kinisa cut the last strawberry and stirred it into a fruit salad. She filled a plastic bowl and sealed it carefully, found her keys, and headed for the door. She took one last look in the mirror and repeated her new name to the unfamiliar face looking back at her. She practiced her opening lines.

"Hello, I am Violet Shepherd."

"Pleased to meet you. I am Violet Shepherd."

With that she set off on her great adventure. With her GPS set, she had no trouble finding Pleasantville or the Lutheran church on the main village drag. She looked for parking and found a lot behind the church. She parked her car and opened her trunk to fetch the fruit salad. A car pulled in next to her and a cheery middle-aged woman hopped out of the driver side. She opened a back door and lifted a casserole from the back seat. She was soon joined by a teenage boy.

"Hi," the woman said. "Are you here for the potluck dinner?"

Pleasantville Lutheran Church
a small community congregation

"Yes, I hope it's OK. I'm new around here and I saw it advertised on your website."

The teenage boy nudged the woman. "I told you the web page was a good idea, Mom."

The woman ignored the remark and kept the attention on Violet. "Well, welcome to Pleasantville Lutheran Church. I'm Carla. This is my son, Earl. If you haven't guessed, he's our web master."

"Pleased to meet you. I am Violet Shepherd."

Ruby relaxed a bit. So far, so good. She had remembered to keep in character. Her first encounter seemed to be going well.

Carla nudged her son. "Earl, be a gentleman."

"Uh, can I help you with anything?" Earl said.

Violet looked the young man over. He reminded her of her own son who had recently left home. She remembered Gil's advice to avoid being the center of attention. "I'm OK, but thanks so much for asking."

Earl started to walk away, but Carla called him back. "How about helping your old mother!" She handed him the casserole, and Earl headed into the church on his own.

"Do you have children?" Carla asked Violet.

"One boy, grown and on his own now," Violet answered honestly.

"Earl's my youngest. I'm glad he's still at home. The other three are in school or recently married. I can't wait for grandkids." Carla continued to chatter as they crossed the large parking lot and neared a back door. "Come on in. I'll introduce you."

Carla held the door and Violet entered a bustling fellowship hall. Three women looked up in greeting.

"There you are. We thought for a minute that Earl made that casserole on his own!" one commented.

The others laughed. "Who's your friend?"

"This is Violet. She saw our web page."

"She did! And we all thought it was a waste," one of the ladies said. "Way to go, Earl!" another shouted.

"Hi, Violet. Welcome. Why don't you sit with us? You'll notice when people start coming in that families stake out their tables. We want you to have plenty of company. You can sit anywhere you like, but feel free to join us 'unaccompanied mothers.'"

Violet couldn't help but smile at the good-natured welcome. She remembered what it was like to go to events with her son and not see him again until it was time to go home. "Unaccompanied mothers" seemed to be an apt description.

She handed someone her fruit salad and found a seat.

Carla sat with Violet.

"So what brings you to Pleasantville?"

Violet thought back to her role-playing with Gil.

"My son found work nearby. I'm looking to relocate near him. I hope to find work, too. Jack is my only family and while I want him to live his own life, I don't want to be too far away. Pleasantville looks like it's close to several sizeable towns."

Violet stopped abruptly, remembering to turn the spotlight on her new acquaintance.

"Tell me about your church. I didn't see the name of a pastor on your website."

"That's right. No pastor," Carla said with no hint of apology. "I'll introduce you to Bob when he comes in. He's the head of our church council. We don't know what we'd do without him!"

Carla and Violet made small talk for a few more minutes when a large man walked in. Carla signaled to him to come over.

"Bob, I want you to meet a guest. This is Violet. She's new to Pleasantville and has been asking questions about our church. She read about us on the new website."

"Welcome, Violet," Bob said. "What can I tell you about Pleasantville Lutheran Church?"

"Well, I'm curious that you don't seem to have a pastor."

"That's right, Violet. We don't have a pastor, and frankly, we don't want one."

Violet tried to hide her surprise. Bob noticed and elaborated.

"We've been without a pastor for nearly three years. The synod tells us no one wants to come here. They sent us supply pastors but they are expensive and aggravating."

Carla interjected. "Looks like Bob is on a roll. Better fasten your seat belt and enjoy the ride."

Bob smiled but didn't miss a beat. "Let me ask you a question. If you were a supply pastor and you knew the service started at 10 a.m., what time would you arrive?"

Violet wasn't sure if the question was rhetorical but she ventured an answer. "9:30, I guess."

"Thank you," Bob said. "We got so tired of supply pastors showing up with barely five minutes before the service. No time for introductions. No time to go over the bulletin. All of us anxious, wondering if anyone would be coming. But let me tell you, they all have their hand out for the check at the last Amen."

Violet was taken aback by Bob's passionate criticism of pastors. "They can't all be like that," she said, trying not to sound defensive.

"Well, there is another kind of supply pastor," Bob continued,— "the one who gives the same sermon over and over again. Gets so we're all sitting in the pews mouthing the words. Anyway, we got to the point that we just thought supply pastors were a drain—to our morale and our bank account. Frankly, things have been going better ever since we decided to provide our own worship leadership. Everybody is chipping in. Carla said you saw our new website. Carla's son, Earl, and one of his school friends put it together. We tried for a year with our last pastor to get a website and got nowhere."

There was no stopping Bob. Neither Carla nor Violet tried.

"You know, the synod thinks that if there's a pastor on the payroll, the church will magically thrive. They know that all we can afford is part-time help, but they expect us to pay that part-timer to do the things we can do ourselves. We expect a pastor to do the things that are difficult for lay people to do — like evening visits, hospital calls and organizing special programs. But the part-timers don't seem to have time for anything but worship. That's not enough to grow a church!"

"So things are going well. What do you do for sermons?" Violet asked. "We take turns giving a message. We have a member who is a retired pastor. If anyone has questions, they turn to him. But, you know, all but a couple of our adult members are college grads. Some have even more schooling. We can read the same sermon tip websites pastors use. Once a month or so, a pastor comes to preside over communion. We even manage without an organist. A member plays electric piano.

If he can't be here, he programs the hymn tunes into the computer. It's not ideal, but we are a busy church that meets its budget. If we weren't operating like this we'd be living beyond our means and synod would probably be trying to close us. As it is, we all pull together, and our membership has been growing."

Violet didn't know what to say. She had no idea that churches like this existed within the synod she had been serving for six years. She wanted to ask more questions, but she didn't want to tip her hand. She just listened.

Bob finally brought the airing of his pet peeves to a close. "Well, if I don't get to work, my better half will be on my tail. Glad you are joining us, Violet. Hope we'll see you on Sunday."

Just as Carla predicted families started to file in and began claiming tables. Violet made a quick estimate and guessed there were about 75.

Most of the adults came by and said hello, pointing out their children who were moving targets in the fellowship hall.

Violet found it easy to relax and enjoy the company of the "unaccompanied mothers." She told them about her son. The other mothers were equally proud of their young people. Violet commented that there seemed to be a good number of youth present.

"We have the Presbyterian Church to thank for that," Carla said. "One of their members invited all the teens from all the churches to form a Service Corps. The young people asked each congregation to submit a proposal for a project that could use the help of young people. The kids all got together and made sure each church got the help they needed."

"What kind of projects?" Violet asked with genuine interest.

"Our congregation asked for the youth to help with Vacation Bible School. It was the first VBS we had in a decade and was very successful." Carla said. "The young people had a blast teaching the younger kids."

"The Baptists asked the youth to renovate an unused room and outfit it as a nursery." another woman added. "Last month they painted the fellowship hall at the Methodist church. Since they pledged to help each church, they all got to know each other really well. Now, they enjoy each other's company. It's not at all unusual to see them at events at all the churches," Carla explained with pride.

"Yes," one of the mothers offered, "I used to have to beg my twins to help out at church. Now they take notice of things their group might be able to help with."

"It's meant the world to us," another mother said. "There was so much that needed to be done that our older people couldn't do. We couldn't afford to pay for the work. We were so concerned that our young people would lose interest. Now they are a big part of our churches — and our community."

Another mother added, "It helped that the youth leader went to the local high school and convinced the school to accept their work to fulfill the school's requirement for community service."

"Earl, my budding entrepreneur, calls it a win-win situation," Carla added with a chuckle. The "unaccompanied mothers" nodded their approval.

But Carla didn't stop there.

"Everybody is happy now, but it would be wrong to suggest it was easy. At first, each congregation suspected the Presbyterians were trying to 'steal' their kids. But the leader met with each church and convinced them that young people like to be together and none of the churches had enough youth to have a vibrant group on their own. If the churches didn't work together all the kids were likely to drop out of church completely. When they got around to starting the Service Corps, he made sure the Presbyterian Church was last on the job list. Otherwise, the young people took control of the projects and set their own priorities."

"Yes, I can only imagine how those meetings with the presbytery went!" one of the women said. The Pleasantville group laughed. They knew she had transferred from the neighboring church when she married years ago. She still had relatives and one foot in the Presbyterian Church.

Violet did not comment, but she was impressed.

After the meal, the youth did a stewardship skit. Carla pointed out that two of the young people were from other neighborhood churches.

Violet truly enjoyed the final activity. One of the older ladies sat down at the piano and played for an old-fashioned sing-along. The song choices were from the 40s, but everyone seemed to be having fun. At one point the young people pulled out some kazoos and hummed along to "Roll Out the Barrel."

Violet returned home and to her old persona with a lot to think about. "Cooperation between churches of the same denomination is hard enough," she thought. "How did they manage to get the whole town involved?"

She looked forward to sharing her experience with Gil Ableman. "Gil won't believe the story I have to tell," she thought.

Pleasantville Lutheran Church
a small community congregation

5
Worship in Pleasantville

Bishop Ruby Kinisa spent a good bit of Saturday reflecting on the Pot Luck Dinner. She was truly impressed with the energy and resourcefulness she found in the Pleasantville congregation. But the lack of a pastor bothered her. She sensed there was more to the story. She looked forward to worshiping with Pleasantville Lutherans on Sunday morning.

She arrived in Pleasantville early the next morning and was not surprised to find Bob preparing the worship area.

"You came back!" he exclaimed when he saw Violet Shepherd walk through the door. "Glad to know I didn't scare you off. My wife scolded me for airing our dirty linen. I'm so sorry to burden you with our problems."

"Not at all, Bob. It shows you care."

Bob handed her a bulletin and quipped, "The first ten pews are reserved for you! Don't worry. You won't be worshiping alone. Our people will be coming in after Sunday School classes end."

Violet entered a nearly empty sanctuary. Two young men were fiddling with the electric piano. They acknowledged Violet's entry with a nod but kept to their business.

Ruby read the bulletin. She noticed that the meditation was to be delivered by a woman with Bob's last name and assumed she was his wife. She looked up the hymns and took note of the variety. True to Bob's word, the sanctuary began to fill as the minute hand began to reach the top of the hour. One of the fellows began to play the piano.

Bob walked to the front of the sanctuary and opened the service with words of welcome. He introduced two women. Yes, the woman who would deliver the sermon was Bob's wife. Carla would be leading the liturgy.

As the opening hymn began, two teens in white cottas came up the aisle and lit the altar candles. That prompted Violet to look

---

around the sanctuary. There was a row of four elementary-aged children sitting by themselves near the front. She recognized a few children sitting with parents from the Potluck.

Attendance appeared to be about the same as on Friday— about 75. Violet made a mental note, "Healthy age mix."

The service went smoothly. Several church members stepped forward to read scriptures and take offerings. Violet was impressed when one young boy, about 10, walked to the front of the church and led unscripted prayer. The meditation followed the lectionary and spoke to the people with appropriate and heartfelt interpretation. As the offering was taken, about seven members of the congregation assembled, a couple with toddlers in tow, and sang a gospel number a cappella.

At the end of the service, Bob made weekly announcements and delivered the benediction. Violet was surprised that he took a moment to introduce her. The congregation applauded with welcome.

As the congregation filed out, Violet found Bob. "Bob, the service was wonderful. I have just one question. How does the synod feel about your lay leadership playing such a significant role?"

"It's a long story, Violet. My wife won't like me telling it. But you asked, and a good question deserves a good answer.

"The synod has been less than encouraging to our congregation. We think they want us to fail, so they can claim our property. The pastors they have sent us for consideration have been unimpressive. This put us between a rock and a hard place. Double our budget and accept a pastor we know is a bad fit and face certain failure—or risk repercussions for doing our own thing and be solely responsible for our own success or failure."

"It looks like you are making things work!" Violet said.

"We've learned a lot! And we have much more to learn! But we are passionate about our ministry. To answer your question more pointedly . . . we don't know how the synod feels about our ministry. They haven't been here in three years. We suspect they don't know much about us."

Violet groped to find something to say, but was speechless.

"I hope our story doesn't discourage you, Violet. We'd love to welcome you into our faith community."

"Well, Bob, my future is a bit uncertain, but I assure you Pleasantville has treated me well."

"It has been our pleasure! Hope we see you again soon. Don't forget to check our website for mid-week activities."

Violet smiled. "Oh, and please tell your wife I'm on Pleasantville's side!"

Ruby drove home from Pleasantville somewhat stunned. Her mind was spinning. "I've been working in the synod office for six years and I never heard this story before." she thought. "All I heard was how small, poor and difficult the Pleasantville congregation is. The bishop back then always said no one wants to go there. I wonder if the candidates met the people the way I did or if they relied on synod reports." Ruby was reminded of Gil's concerns about prejudice.

Bishop Kinisa's concern for the good people of Pleasantville made her all the more eager for her next visit.

6
The Sidekick

Gil called Bishop Kinisa first thing Monday morning. Ruby was excited to talk.

"I visited Pleasantville yesterday. All I can say is 'Wow!'" she said. "I didn't even have to ask questions. Boy, did I get an earful!"

"I'm guessing you met Bob Forster, then."

"How did you know?"

"Bob gave your predecessor a tough time—or vice versa. The bishop wanted Pleasantville to accept a pastor he was having a hard time placing. He gave the congregation an ultimatum. 'Call this pastor or else.' Bob—and the rest of Pleasantville's council—would have none of it. The bishop even tried to bypass the church council. He insisted the congregation vote, hoping they'd vote against the recommendation of their own leaders. But the congregation supported their council. Pleasantville went its own way. The bishop never backed away from his threat. He quietly cut them from the list of congregations seeking pastoral help. It's been like that for quite a while. Not many know they have no pastor. How are things in Pleasantville? I often wonder."

"Things look like they are going very well. I'm glad for them, but it doesn't make us look very good. The congregation is small but active. I wanted to ask them why they don't support the synod, but Violet wouldn't ask that kind of question."

"Isn't it obvious, Ruby? Would you support an organization that isn't helping you and which actually wrote you off? You know, I always admired Bob Forster. At times, I had to remind myself I worked for the synod. He made a lot of sense and worked incredibly hard for his church. I was always rooting for him. Now I wish I'd spoken up for him."

"Gil, I've sat in on many committee meetings discussing synod finances. Congregations like Pleasantville are always presented as if they are dying—beyond hope."

Gil asked, "Is the lack of parish reporting starting to make sense?"

"I guess so."

"Where's your next visit?"

"I'm thinking of visiting Zion in the Riverside neighborhood in the city next weekend. Meanwhile, I'm changing my mind about being out of the office so long. I'd better stop by the salon, pick up my wig, and make an appearance tomorrow."

"Good idea! The natives are a bit restless!" Gil joked.

Ruby was glad she made time to go into the office the next day. There were 1000 emails and a stack of phone call messages to return. Pam, her secretary, helped her prioritize them. Ruby reminded herself that she was new to all this. She enjoyed watching Pam take charge.

Late in the afternoon, Gil came to her door. "I have someone for you to meet," he said, as he directed a youthful-looking, middle-aged man through the threshold.

"Bishop Kinisa, this is Bruce James. I mentioned him to you last week. He's finishing his last seminary obligations. I thought he'd be perfect to help you with your project."

"Good to meet you, Bruce. Please, both of you, come in and shut the door behind you." Ruby picked up the intercom and asked Pam to hold calls.

"Good to meet you, Bishop," Bruce said. "Gil has been a bit secretive. What's this all about?"

"As you know, I was just elected to this office. Gil, being the ranking veteran around here, has been helping me review the parish reports. Frankly, I've found them to be disturbing. We want to find answers to a lot of questions, but Gil advised me that the bishop doesn't always get straight answers."

"How so?" Bruce asked.

"I defer to Gil. He is older and wiser," Ruby said with a wink.

Gil took over. "I just pointed out to Bishop Kinisa that pastors often tell the bishop what they think he or she wants to hear. After all, they have self-interest. They don't want to put up any roadblocks in their career paths."

The bishop added. "I decided to visit congregations incognito in hopes of learning more about their challenges. I've visited one church so far and the experience was humbling, to say the least."

"Tell me more." Bruce asked with growing curiosity.

"I have begun to see lay leadership in a new light. I hate to say it, but all this time I have unconsciously viewed lay Christians as 'assistants to the pastors.' My first visit revealed that they can be the driving engine."

"Interesting!" Bruce said.

Ruby noticed Gil's restlessness. "What is it, Gil?"

"Well, it's taken me my whole career to realize this, but lay leaders bring a lot of experience to the table. Bruce, you are about to be ordained. You've worked in the secular sector for what, twenty years?"

"Just about," Bruce answered.

"How active were you in church during that time?"

Bruce stuttered. "Uh, I attended worship fairly regularly, but I was on the road a lot. I tried to help with mission projects when my children were in youth group."

"Did you attend Bible Study? Did you teach Sunday School? Did you sing in the choir? Were you on the Church Council?"

"Uh, sorry to say, I was pretty busy with my job and family."

"Bruce, when you accept your first call, you will be working side by side with lay people who spent those twenty years leading their church. Collectively—and in many cases individually— they will have more experience than you."

Ruby said nothing but mentally compared her five years' experience as an associate pastor with that of Bob Forster and his wife.

Bruce admitted, "I never thought of it that way. But I get your point. This project sounds ambitious. Why are you talking with an inexperienced guy like me?"

Gil answered. "Bishop Kinisa has already started her visits. She has an amazing disguise, by the way. But we think some of the pastors will know her if they start talking with her. In those cases, we thought she should visit with a partner who could manage the direct interface. You are graduating from a seminary fairly distant from us. Clergy are not likely to recognize you."

Ruby interrupted. "Bruce, the fact is we don't know what we are doing. But I am determined to connect with the people in the pew. I don't like fooling people, but I don't know any other way to get to the truth."

"Count me in!" Bruce said.

The three chatted for an hour, discussing strategy.

Finally, the intercom buzzed. "Sorry to interrupt, but it is after 5 o'clock and I need to leave," Pam said. "Everyone else is gone."

"Thanks, Pam. We'll be right behind you."

She turned to Bruce. "Come with me on Sunday. We can go in the same car, if you don't mind meeting me at my apartment."

"I'll be there with bells on!"

7
Zion in the City

Bruce arrived at Bishop Kinisa's apartment and rang the bell. When Violet answered in Ruby's stead, Bruce started to apologize, but Violet put him out of his misery.

"You don't recognize me, do you?" she asked, quite proud of herself.

Bruce gasped and then started laughing. "Gil said you have a great disguise!"

"Let's get going!" She glanced toward the parking lot. "Looks like you are parked right beside me."

Ruby grilled him on the forty-minute drive into the city. "What's my name again?"

"Violet Shepherd."

"Who are you?"

"I'm your old friend, Jim Bruce."

"I looked in Zion's file and I see that Zion has an interim minister," the bishop said. "That means he was working closely with my predecessor, so he will probably be hoping to meet with me soon. We need to be playing our 'A' Game."

They reached Zion comfortably early. They looked for a parking lot, found none, but easily found parking on the street. As they were locking the car door, a woman walked by. She was well dressed, obviously headed for worship.

"Are you joining us today?" she asked as she passed.

"As a matter of fact, we are." Jim Bruce said.

"Follow me," the woman said cheerfully. "I'm Rosetta Gorton."

Jim continued to take the lead. "This is my friend, Violet Shepherd. I'm Jim Bruce. We're sightseeing and thought we'd start our day in the city by visiting your historic church."

Ruby smiled at the way Bruce had adjusted his moniker.

"Great! We're proud of our roots. We are the oldest Lutheran church in the state. Five other city churches grew from our early mission work and countless more from that. Let me introduce you to our sexton. He'll give you a tour."

Rosetta took them inside and signaled to the sexton. "Andy, these visitors would like a tour, can you help them, please?"

"Glad to, but worship is about to start. Meet me at the back of the church after the service. Oh, and welcome."

Rosetta led them into the sanctuary; made sure they had a bulletin and guided them to a seat behind a row where three older women were sitting with their jackets and tote bags sprawled beside them.

Rosetta whispered, "Zion's finest seniors will be glad to help if you have any trouble."

On cue, each of the ladies turned around, nodded in silent greeting and looked them over. One said, "Everything is in the bulletin."

Violet and Jim settled back and listened to a piano prelude. She was glad Rosetta had seated them toward the rear. She could get a good look at the congregation and she was farther from the pulpit.

As the first chords of the opening hymn began, Violet counted about 35 people. Then she heard strong voices behind her. A choir of about eight began to file up the center aisle. At the end of the double column was Pastor Patrick Meyers, the interim pastor.

As the hymn ended, Pastor Meyers stepped to the center of the chancel. "I have just a few announcements," he said. Violet's attention drifted as he ran down the list of parish activities. Her ears perked when Pastor announced that he planned to visit the bishop this week to review the progress Zion was making in their interim ministry.

"I'm sure Pam was planning to tell me," she thought.

The service began. Violet took another head count. More had drifted in. She began to analyze the assemblage. The most noticeable thing about the group was that there was not a single child. There were a few youth, sitting together, some young adults sitting alone, as well as a few middle-aged couples.

Most were elderly.

The service moved smoothly and soon Pastor Meyers began his sermon. He gave an energetic message and then he posed a few questions. Violet was surprised that he instructed the congregation to discuss the questions and retreated to a chancel seat.

The row of elderly ladies turned to Violet and Jim and explained apologetically. "He's young. He's into this new stuff." Another added, "He's here just one year. We don't have him trained yet." The third grumbled, "He thinks, we are discussing his sermon. We're not."

Violet had a hard time keeping from laughing. "A row of loyal critics," she thought. She was pleased to see Pastor Meyers' efforts. She made a mental note to compliment him—when the time was right.

Bruce didn't let the opportunity to talk go by. "How do you really feel about your pastor?" he asked with a twinkle in his eye.

The ladies seemed to appreciate the question and immediately became more engaging.

"He's not our pastor. He's our interminable interim."

Violet nearly choked. But Bruce was in the driver's seat. "How long has he been here?"

"A little more than a year with no end in sight."

"I thought interims were to help with transitions in ministry."

"That's what we thought, too."

Another added, "We are asked to jump through one hoop after another. It's like they think we can't do anything without him!"

The first lady continued. "We're waiting for something to happen . . . and it never happens. Don't get us wrong. He's a nice guy. But people don't want to form a relationship just to have him leave as soon as *he* thinks it's time. We miss Pastor Gottlund, but more than that, we miss having a pastor. The younger people don't know anyone but Pastor Gottlund. They are tired of being in limbo and are starting to look around. They're not like us old gals. We complain. But at least we come. Others stop coming."

Another lady spoke up. "Pastor Gottlund was here for twenty years. We old folks can remember plenty of transitions before him that didn't require a full-time babysitter."

Violet took it all in. She had never heard interim ministry described this way.

Just then Pastor Meyers returned to the pulpit and drew his sermon to a close.

After church, Jim Bruce and Violet Shepherd attempted to talk with him. After a few niceties, he excused himself to talk with a council leader. Violet noted that he had not mentioned taking church members with him to his visit with the bishop. She began to look forward to seeing him in her office.

Meanwhile, Andy, the sexton, came to them and began his tour. He started outside at the cornerstone.

He pointed to three dated stones. Two had been salvaged from earlier buildings. He explained that the current sanctuary was actually a chapel. They climbed a steep stairs into a much grander worship area.

Both Jim and Violet viewed the beautiful sanctuary in awe, but they were puzzled to see a table saw set up in the center aisle. The sexton explained that the congregation was selling off the pews to make money. They didn't foresee using the large space for worship anytime soon. It was expensive to heat and a cavernous atmosphere for their small number of people.

Violet ventured a question now that the interim pastor wasn't present. "Is your congregation growing?"

"Hard to say. People aren't leaving, but they aren't coming out for this new guy like they did for Pastor Gottlund. We really want a pastor and soon. A year is a long time to live under synod's constant scrutiny. We get visitors, but when they learn the pastor is short-term, they tend to keep moving."

Andy went on to show them the classroom space, now used for daycare. Violet was full of questions but knew the two "visitors" could ask only so much and maintain their cover.

They thanked Andy. Violet spotted Rosetta, talking in the corner. She caught her eye, mouthed a thank you and waved good-bye.

The ride home was a bit somber. Both Bruce and Ruby felt the pall hanging over this congregation.

"What a contrast from Pleasantville," she thought. It troubled her that the gloom seemed to be the interim ministry. Ruby told Bruce that the synod was proud of its interim program. It was supposed to help congregations plan ministry with a new pastor. She had never considered any "downside."

She couldn't wait to talk things over with Gil. He'd been in on the interim program from the beginning.

8
Interim Troubles

Gil Ableman walked through the maze of office cubicles singing in his rich baritone voice the old hymn.

"O Zion, haste, thy mission high fulfilling,
to tell to all the world that God is light..."

The synod staff grinned as he passed. They were used to Gil's style. He had a hymn for every occasion!

No one wondered what prompted this particular rendition. It was just Gil being Gil.

He reached Bishop Kinisa's door and stood squarely in the threshold. "So how are things at Zion, Riverside?"

Ruby lost no time. "Come in, Gil. We need to talk."

Gil sobered quickly. "What happened?"

"Bruce and I found a congregation in— I don't know— depression—and I think it's our fault."

"Are things not going well with Pat Meyers? I think he's one of our best."

"Things aren't going well, but I don't think Pat is the problem. I've done little but think about this since yesterday morning. Gil, I think what's wrong is the whole interim ministry concept."

"How can you fault the concept?" Gil asked. "An interim minister goes in after a pastor retires or leaves to take another call. The interim resolves any issues resulting from the change in leadership and helps the congregation draft new mission and vision statements in preparation for a new leader."

"It sounds good. I'm not sure where this good concept is going wrong. I checked with Pam this morning and Pastor Meyers is coming here to meet on Thursday afternoon. We'll learn more then. I'd like you to sit in, please. Meanwhile, all I can tell you is that Bruce and I encountered a congregation that is withering in the interim process. For all the emphasis on 'new direction' the people are feeling rudderless and powerless. While we seem content when an 'interim' is in place, the congregation is overwhelmed with a sense of—I don't know—'stagnation' might be the word."

"That does sound troubling," Gil confessed. "We started the interim program with the best of intentions—as I'm sure you know. You placed some interims in your territory, didn't you."

"A few. I was following my predecessor's policies. It seemed like a good idea to create a buffer between pastorates. Often a sudden change in leadership results in conflict that could cripple a new pastor. We were trying to find a way to make transitions go more smoothly. I am beginning to suspect that our idea of smooth transition may have little to do with church members' ideas. But let's hold off dissecting our work until we have a chance to talk to Pat. Maybe we should talk to some other interims, as well."

Gil thought for a moment. "Maybe we should talk to church members, too."

9
Time for A Call

On Thursday afternoon, Pam escorted the Rev. Patrick Meyers into Bishop Ruby Kinisa's office. She and Gil Ableman were already seated at a small conference table. Bishop Kinisa welcomed Pastor Meyers and invited him to join them at the table.

"I know this is a bit awkward," Ruby began. "You are the expert on helping congregations in transition. Today you find yourself facing transition."

"I guess," Pat said with a smile. "I last sat at this table with your predecessor. How do we begin?"

Gil spoke first. "Tell us about your work with Zion. How is it going?"

"Zion is doing just fine. There really isn't much more for me to do as far as preparing the congregation. Pastor Gottlund was a wonderful pastor. I never met him, but he has become a mentor to me. He worked with the congregation for years to prepare them for his retirement. I think they are ready to call a pastor any day. I feel almost guilty that I was promised a position there for 18 months."

Ruby swallowed hard. "Are you saying you were assigned to Zion for 18 months."

"That was my understanding." Pat said. "The previous bishop had a call in mind for me in about two years. The pastor at Trinity, Longtown, is due to retire. It's near our home and my wife's work. Our boys won't have to change schools. He asked me to wait out the time by helping Zion. I hope that's still the plan."

Ruby tapped her pencil on the table, wondering if Trinity knew their next pastor had already been chosen for them and if any interim process there was intended.

Gil continued the questioning. "Is there a signed term call at Zion, then?"

"Zion signed a term-call for eighteen months at the insistence of the bishop. They didn't want an interim for that long. To tell you the truth, they weren't keen on the idea of an interim at all. The bishop insisted. Anyway, the bishop assured me that the term call was flexible and I could stay until a call became available in my area."

"Let's talk about Zion for a minute," Ruby suggested. "How were things when you went there?"

"Not bad. They were sorry to see Pastor Gottlund leave but their leadership handled it well. They held a series of events that helped them say good-bye. There was no conflict, if that's what you are asking."

"How about the congregation's leadership. Is there a sense of direction?"

"One thing I've learned in my year with Zion is that there is always a sense of direction. They have strong lay leadership that is alert to problems and opportunities and brings good ideas to the table. They know their neighborhood and are very involved. They welcome the participation of new people. Really, Zion is a great church. I wouldn't mind serving it, except I'm ineligible by virtue of being their interim."

Ruby continued. "I am surprised that you came in by yourself. Couldn't the council leadership come with you?"

"Uh, I confess I didn't ask them. The last bishop always met with me alone during the day when lay members are busy."

Both Gil and Ruby paused.

Finally, Ruby spoke. "Pat, we are thinking of seriously looking at the interim ministry program with a mind for overhauling it. I have always liked the concept, but it seems that somewhere along the line the train has derailed."

"I hope it isn't anything I've done," Pat Meyers said with concern. "I'm feeling a bit blind-sided."

"I'm not looking to place blame. I think you are a good pastor. But it does concern me that your ministry at Zion seems to be about keeping you busy more than it is about Zion's needs. If Zion is as ready for a pastor as you indicate, it is time to help them find a pastor."

"Zion is ready. But I have a contract that I and my family are counting on."

Bishop Kinisa assured Pastor Meyers that his interests would be protected but that he should not expect to stay at Zion beyond the 18 months. Furthermore, if a promising candidate for pastor was found and Zion issued a call, his contract would be filled in different ways.

"This is what I'd like to see happen," Ruby directed. "I'd like you to return here in two weeks and bring Zion's council leaders with you. It's time the people were part of the congregational evaluation process."

"I serve at your pleasure," Pastor Meyers said, his tone revealing his concern. "I will make an appointment with Pam as I leave."

"Ask Pam for some open evening appointments. Ask Zion's leaders to choose one that works for them. Tell Pam you'll be calling to confirm a time on Monday. I'll be glad to come to Zion or your group can come here. From now on, we pastors will serve at the congregation's pleasure." Bishop Kinisa stressed.

Pastor Meyers left sheepishly but did exactly as the bishop suggested.

Gil and Ruby powwowed.

Gil said, "I should have been more alert to what was happening. Since you told me about your visit at Zion, I've been looking through the records. It takes some reading between the lines, but there is evidence that interim ministries have become tools for the placement of clergy more than for the benefit of congregations. I still like the concept. But it is clear to me that it is being abused."

"You're right, Gil. And churches are suffering. My experiences at Pleasantville and Zion—two churches I chose randomly—reveal that NEWS Synod has been acting as an employment agency for clergy. The interests of the congregations have been secondary. Gil, this is going to change," Ruby stressed.

"The problem is that if interim pastors are doing well, they are working their way out of a job. They are not paid when they are not serving a church. That is creating a conflict of interest, which we just witnessed," Gil said.

Ruby began to speak, her passion rising with every word. "The interim pastor process began as being driven by the congregation with involvement of congregational leadership. The interim was chosen and called by the congregation. NEWS has been assigning interims, which gives them an aura of 'working for the synod.' The congregations are stuck in a process with little control, short of bucking the bishop and risking being 'written off' like Pleasantville. NEWS Synod is slowly self-destructing."

"Changing this isn't going to be easy, Ruby. A lot of clergy have come to expect assignments based on *their* needs. We have 50 clergy trained as interim ministers. We need places for them to serve. You are likely to face resistance. Remember, the clergy account for an influential third of a synod vote."

"More when you consider that much of the remaining two thirds is following their lead," Ruby was surprised to hear herself say.

"Gil, how can we talk to our congregations about mission if we are derelict about our own mission? The synod exists to serve congregations. Pastors serve congregations. Calls come from congregations. They aren't designed for the convenience of clergy. Our comfort and security is secondary to the needs of the congregations, which, by the way, we expect will pay our bills. We are losing our sense of purpose. I have seen it with my own eyes. We have to make this synod work better for the congregations. I intend to begin with the interim process."

"OK, Bishop," Gil said with respect. "The statistics agree with you. I'm with you all the way. Do you and Bruce have plans for Sunday?"

"Bruce and I are driving out to Grace, Center Township, on Sunday."

10
Grace in the Country

Bishop Ruby Kinisa and Bruce James (alias Violet Shepherd and Jim Bruce) set out early for Center Township. They expected to drive at least an hour, hoping for light Sunday morning traffic.

Ruby shared what little she knew of Grace. It was an old country church that was slowly being swallowed by the suburbs. It sat in the middle of a green field across from housing developments. Few pastoral candidates had shown any interest in the congregation and they seemed to get by with short-term pastors and supplies. There were larger churches of various denominations nearby with new buildings to attract newcomers to the area. The congregation was largely out of touch with the synod, being one of the most remote congregations from synod headquarters.

They found the church with ease. As they stood along the country road, facing the wooden church building, the word "quaint" came to mind. There were a few cars parked on the grass nearby, but

Grace in the Country

the two visitors didn't expect to see many people when they entered. The large doors opened to a small narthex and meeting hall. There were steps flanking the entrance, which they guessed would lead to a sanctuary.

They were surprised to see a boy, about 12, sitting at a desk inside the door.

"You're new!" the boy said, more as a matter of fact than greeting. "Do you want to meet the pastor?"

Just then, a gray-haired man wearing a clerical collar came down one of the stairs. "Alex, do we have visitors?"

Remembering their cover, Ruby made the introductions. "Good morning, I'm Violet and this is my friend, Jim."

The man turned to the boy and said, "Alex, you make the introductions."

Alex took direction well. "I'm Alex and this is Pastor Mintner."

Pastor Mintner took over. "Good morning. We are glad to see you here at Grace today."

Ruby didn't recognize Pastor Mintner as a rostered pastor, which concerned her, but she remembered her role as visitor. "Thank you. The sanctuary is up the stairs, I'm guessing."

"Yes, these old churches are built for the healthy," Pastor Mintner replied. "It was more important to our founders that worship be held as close to heaven as we can get — even if we have trouble getting there. Seriously, there is a chairlift," he pointed out.

Violet and Jim climbed the stairs and were surprised to see a great deal of activity. Near the front, were about eight children, ages five to twelve, scattered in two rows. Two women were sitting near the center of the sanctuary with four children. Two men were sitting on the opposite side of the church. Near the back, the pews were full, including one row of older women. On the other side was a cluster of youth. Couples and singles were scattered. A woman greeted them and handed them a colorful bulletin.

"Welcome to Grace. We are glad you are joining us for worship.

I'd like to invite you to stay afterwards for fellowship. Two of our teens are hosting today. They made soup."

"Why, thank you," Violet answered. "What a nice invitation. We will be sure to join you."

The visitors were forced to find seats farther front than usual. The organist was already playing classical preludes.

When the organist stopped, a woman, leaning heavily on an arm-braced crutch, came forward. "Let's begin our worship with a few praise songs." A young man appeared and began strumming a guitar.

The congregation sang strongly, following the words in the bulletin. Violet was jolted at the contrast from the classical repertoire of the organist, but the congregation seemed to take it in stride. After about three hymns—two well known and one fairly modern— the woman pointed to the cover of the bulletin and asked the congregation to read together a poem that accompanied a modern piece of art.

At the end of the poem, the organist began playing the opening hymn. Pastor Mintner entered from the side sacristy. He was wearing a suit with just a stole across his shoulders.

The rest of the service went smoothly.

After the Gospel, the children came forward. Violet and Jim were ready for a standard children's sermon but were surprised when a teenage boy came forward and began talking to the children. He asked them to retell the Gospel story that had just been read.

The children obviously knew the routine. They excitedly retold the Gospel in their own words. They were quick to correct one another if they strayed. The boy asked some good questions about the story. The children gave thoughtful answers. The boy called to the guitarist and asked him to play a song. The children sang along with physical enthusiasm. When the song was over, one of the children shouted, "Again!" And the guitarist obliged. They sang the song two more times, the children never tiring and the adults joining in.

The boy asked for a request and the children shouted the names of two or three favorites. The boy chose one. Finally, the boy asked, "Whose turn is it to lead us in prayer?" The children pointed to one of the youngest girls. "Katie's turn!" Katie folded her hands and said a prayer, her voice barely audible to human ears, but with a great deal of confidence for a pre-schooler. The boy called the children's session over.

"Now Pastor Mintner is going to give a sermon. I want you to count the number of times he says the word 'love.'"

The children rushed back to their seats. The sermon began. Violet and Jim found themselves counting the word "love" along with the children.

As prayers were offered, several in the congregation offered petitions—two in foreign languages.

Violet and Jim were surprised to hear someone in the congregation playing flute along with the last hymn.

After church, the congregation filed down the stairs to the fellowship hall, where two girls were serving chicken soup. About 40 people crowded around tables grouped together. Violet noticed that people filled in the closest seats rather than grouping as families.

Pastor Mintner sat with Violet and Jim and began asking them questions. Jim fielded the answers according to their usual script.

"This is one of the most eclectic worship services I've ever attended," Violet commented.

"Grace is an eclectic church," Pastor Mintner said. "Some people might call us misfits. Every person here has a story. Most have felt excluded by the world, even by the church."

The thought disturbed Violet. "Excluded? How?"

"Well, take the boy who greeted you at the door. Alex is a special needs student. He first came to Grace as part of our nursery program. He'll tell you this is his home. He is teased at school — and life isn't easy for him at home. The people of Grace took him under their wing. There was a time when he barely spoke. They gave him that little desk. It makes him feel important. He is playing a bigger role at Grace all the time. He can shine here. He is the first one to arrive every Sunday morning and he comes alone.

"Then there's Helen. She led the singing. She gets by on disability. She's been crippled since childhood. She tries to find work, but employers take one look at her crutch and awkward movement and move on. At Grace, she's known for her abilities. She is quite a leader.

"The children you saw sitting by themselves—they are kids from the Section 8 housing on the edge of town. Their moms work Sunday morning. They show up here every week.

"We have a few immigrant families. You may have noticed that the women sit with the children on one side of the church and the men sit together on the other side. As I said, everyone at Grace has a story—a story of grace."

Jim smiled. "Now you sound like a preacher."

Violet commented, "I can't help but wonder how you can survive—a church made up of children, teens, a few families and elderly."

"Grace is blessed in so many ways. We have a healthy endowment. If no one contributed a penny, we could get by for twenty more years. But people do contribute. We have a small income from a day-care program. We are not rich but we are happy."

"I can see that," Violet said.

Both Violet and Jim were eager to ask many more questions, but held back.

"What do you see in the future?" Jim asked casually.

Pastor Minter answered, "I have no crystal ball, but every five or ten years, the synod tries to either close Grace or force it to merge with a church five miles away. 'More cost effective,' they say. Every time they do that it upsets the church and sets us back. We always manage to recover, but it makes it hard to attract leadership. Pastors know the synod has designs and they steer clear. People hesitate to give, wondering if the synod intends to take their offerings.

"The truth is, the members of Grace would be lost in any merger. Our people would be unchurched. Most have no transportation. The things that hold us back in society would likely limit—if not exclude us—from full participation in a larger church. Grace is our spiritual lifeline."

Jim noticed that the Pastor always included himself as a member of the church, saying "we" and "us." He liked that.

"How did you come to Grace?" Jim asked.

"I'm retired, rostered in the neighboring synod. My family has roots here. I returned for homecoming a couple of years ago. I was so impressed that I offered to help. I've been filling their pulpit as a supply for nearly two years. I think things are going pretty well, but I invite you to talk to our members. Their opinion counts more than mine. Let me introduce you."

Pastor Mintner called on several members, who lifted their bowls of soup and moved closer to Violet and Jim.

On the ride home, Bruce commented, "Everyone was so easy to talk to. I felt like I was sitting at Sunday dinner in their dining room."

Ruby couldn't help but have concerns, but she had to admit Grace offered inspirational worship. The tune the children sang kept repeating in her mind.

11
Sufficient Grace

Gil Ableman and Ruby were having their usual Monday strategy session. Ruby was eager to talk about the visit to Grace, including both the things she liked and the few things that concerned her. "So how are things in Center Township?" Gil opened.

"Fascinating place! What do you know about this Pastor Mintner?" Ruby asked.

"John Mintner? Nice guy. Good pastor."

"You know him then? He's not rostered with us."

"John's an alien, all right. Your predecessor treated him like one, too, I'm sorry to say. John approached the bishop two or three years ago about serving Grace. The bishop paid no attention to him. John persisted—writing letters, calling, and even stopping by the office. The bishop, I think, was trying to discourage him. He didn't want to help Grace, if they weren't going to take his advice. I think he thought if he ignored them, they would appear in his office on their knees, begging for synod help, and then he'd have an opening to force them to close or at least get that endowment under synod control."

"Doesn't look like the plan is working? Grace is a lively place."

"That doesn't surprise me," Gil said. "I went to seminary with John. He is a dedicated parish pastor. Grace may pay him something, but he is largely volunteering. He may have transferred his membership. There is some family connection. I think his grandparents may have been members. Anyway, since John was a member of the congregation, the bishop didn't really have the power to oust him and so Grace did its thing and NEWS Synod paid no attention."

"That endowment keeps coming up. John mentioned it, too."

"Yes, that was part of the problem. The bishop was upset that they received an endowment. He had other plans for the parish. He wanted to merge it with St. Peter's, a good five miles away. The endowment gave Grace independence. The church council voted down his proposal. Your predecessor's style was to walk away when congregations didn't agree with him. John has been holding things together, as far as I can tell."

"The ministry there is unusual, but everyone seems to get along. Children from the neighborhood without their parents, immigrants, elderly, disabled, a good number of teens, families, singles. Their worship was artistic. Poetry. Music, Art, Storytelling. People were really involved, too."

"That's John's influence, I'm guessing. They've always had strong lay leadership, too. Strong enough to say 'no' to the last bishop —and probably a few before him."

"I'm trying to figure out how to help them and tap their energy to help other small churches. They are definitely filling a need. I'd almost call them a 'mission' church."

"Watch out!" Gil warned. "That term is a red flag to churches like Grace. Synod's view has been a 'mission' church exists only under synodical leadership. Declaring a church a 'mission church' is a way of taking control of the congregation. It's hard to argue against the concept of 'mission.' But in many cases, giving a congregation mission status was a foot in the door for eventual closure and permanent control of a congregation's assets. That's doesn't fly with churches that have a good self-image and the skills to do the work. When they fail to agree with synod's plan for them, they risk being cut off from full participation in NEWS Synod."

"Is that what happened at Grace?"

"You got it! It created a bitter conflict at the time and lasting enmity. Grace wanted to reach out to their changing neighborhood, but they wanted to influence their own ministry. NEWS responded by sending in consultants—at considerable expense to the congregation, I might add. The consultants, not surprisingly, supported synod's view of Grace's ministry potential — or lack of it. The congregation felt hoodwinked.

"It's been years, but there is a definite lack of trust between the synod and Grace. The synod didn't trust Grace's ability to forge its own ministry and Grace suspected the synod had a hidden agenda in trying to force it into 'mission' status. I hope your undercover operation doesn't add to the distrust."

"Gil, I went undercover to find out what no one would tell me. I think it's working. I'm getting an earful! Now the trick will be to turn what I'm learning into something good, something that pleases the Lord. I can recall now discussions about congregations like Grace here at NEWS Synod headquarters. Now I realize I heard only one side of a complex story."

"That's true," Gil said. "It's a mess that's going to be difficult to clean up. For one thing, word is out among the pastors to steer clear of congregations like Grace. There is a stigma to serving these parishes, and there are a few of them. That's why I advised you to look for congregations that had no pastor or very limited pastoral help."

Gil thought for a moment about his own role in this scenario.

"May I make a suggestion?" he offered at last.

"Sure! We're in this together."

"You need to return to each church and ask just one question:

How can NEWS Synod help you in your ministry?

No threats. No force. Hands off the endowments—your ears and heart truly open to what the people have to say. Let them do the talking." Gil stopped and took a deep breath. "I've been waiting a long time to get that off my chest."

"I suspect you are right. It is time for humility. I'm glad I have a good mentor."

"I assume you are talking about Christ," Gil said.

"Him, too." Ruby smiled.

Pleasantville Lutheran Church
a small community congregation

12
Studying Philippians in Pleasantville

Violet went by herself to the Bible Study in Pleasantville, the small town congregation with no pastor. She did not know what to expect — only that the website said the topic was Philippians. She entered a well-lit side door. The sound of voices led her to a small room furnished with overstuffed chairs. Six women looked up when she entered. Violet recognized Bob Forster's wife. She had not been introduced but Violet remembered she had given the meditation during worship.

"Why, it's Violet. I remember you. You visited a few weeks ago. My husband, Bob, chewed your ear, I'm afraid. I'm Martha. Welcome."

"Glad to meet you, Martha. By the way, I enjoyed your meditation that morning. I was curious about your congregation's Bible study. I saw on your website that you have two."

"Yes. The young mothers have a group that meets while their children have playtime. They go to different homes. They would have a hard time coming out in the evening for Bible Study. But we compare notes after church."

"Sounds like a good idea," Violet said. "Different strokes for different folks. Are you still studying Philippians?" Violet asked.

"We're finishing the book tonight. Have a seat, Violet. We're so glad you are joining us."

Martha made quick introductions. The group went straight to work. "Here's how we operate. We take turns leading the Bible study. It's my turn tonight. We read passages together. The leader does some research online so she can point out a thing or two. Then we discuss. We sing a hymn and finish with prayer. Don't be shy! We're not! Now, let's get started."

The ladies bowed their heads in silence for a few seconds.

"Well, ladies, we are on Chapter 4 of the book of Philippians. I can tell you straight up that Paul takes care of some housekeeping in this chapter. In between the 'thank yous,' 'good-byes' and 'take cares,' he talks about peace.

The ladies took turns reading. They seemed to have a rhythm, knowing naturally when to stop for the next to begin. Violet took a turn, too. She read verses 8 and 9:

> *Finally, brothers and sisters, whatever is true, whatever*
> *is noble, whatever is right, whatever is pure, whatever is*
> *lovely, whatever is admirable—if anything is excellent or*
> *praiseworthy—think about such things. Whatever you have*
> *learned or received or heard from me, or seen in me—put it*
> *into practice. And the God of peace will be with you.*

Violet stopped and the next reader began, but Violet's thoughts remained on this passage. "Think about the good," she reminded herself.

Martha thanked all the readers and asked for some impressions from the group.

I heard the benediction in there, one woman said.

"That would be verse 7," Martha said.

Another commented on the mention of Caesar's household. Martha was ready with some information about the military community in Philippi.

Another commented on Paul's regard for the women in the community. They talked about the role of women in the church. "Sometimes it takes a woman to see what's really needed," one commented. "Paul said it was their church that sent him support when no one else did. I hope our new bishop sees the needs in our churches and does something."

Violet swallowed hard.

After a lengthy discussion, Martha interrupted. "Since this is the last week of our Bible Study on Philippians, let's recap the other chapters. Grab a partner and form three groups. I'll give you a couple of minutes. Pick out a key thought from chapters 1, 2, and 3. Just one thought from each chapter to remind us of our discussions.

> Group 1 read from Chapter 1: *And this is my prayer: that your love may abound more and more in knowledge and depth of insight, so that you may be able to discern what is best and may be pure and blameless for the day of Christ, filled with the fruit of righteousness that comes through Jesus Christ—to the glory and praise of God.*

> Group 2 read from Chapter 2: *Do nothing out of selfish ambition or vain conceit. Rather, in humility value others above yourselves, not looking to your own interests but each of you to the interests of the others.*

> Group 3 read from Chapter 3: *But our citizenship is in heaven. And we eagerly await a Savior from there, the Lord Jesus Christ, who, by the power that enables him to bring everything under his control, will transform our lowly bodies so that they will be like his glorious body.*

Violet was part of Group 3, but somehow she felt that each chosen verse was directed toward her. She couldn't help but wonder if her cover was broken.

While Violet's mind wrestled with the Bible passages, Martha began leading a spirited rendition of "Peace Like A River."

At last, all the women stood, joined hands, and took turns praying.

Violet returned to her world refreshed and humbled.

13
Zion in the City Revisited

Having restored her normal appearance, Ruby went into the office a bit early the next day and found her secretary, Pam, busy shuffling papers and clearing her desk.

"Good morning, Bishop," Pam greeted Ruby. "I hope you are ready for work. Things have been piling up. If there was any honeymoon in your first few weeks as bishop, I declare it to be officially over!"

Ruby laughed. "Just take things one at a time," she advised. "What's hot?"

"Well, Pastor Meyers from Zion has been calling. He wants you to visit his church this week. He sounds stressed."

"Did he suggest a time and place?"

"Yes. He said Tuesday evening or Thursday evening at 7 pm at Zion would work for his people."

"Confirm for Tuesday and let Gil know, too. I want him to come with me."

"The next Tuesday evening, Gil and Bishop Kinisa, complete with wig, returned to Zion and were met at the door by Pastor Patrick Meyers, the congregation's interim pastor."

Ruby noticed his discomfort and tried to put him at ease. "Pat, I know you've been doing a good job here. Remember, I'm new at my job. Gil has been helping me learn more about the congregations. This meeting is more about me learning about Zion than about you and your work. I'm sure you can understand that I want to move things in the best direction. I'm counting on you to be part of that effort."

Her words had a calming effect. The pastor escorted them to a meeting room, where eight people were sitting around a conference table.

"Members of Zion Council, I am pleased to introduce our new bishop, the Rev. Ruby Kinisa and the Rev. Gil Ableman of NEWS Synod.

The council stood, each extending a hand in welcome. Each gave a name. Ruby recognized two of them—

Rosetta Gorton and Andy, the sexton.

"Please, everyone, let's all sit down," Pastor Meyers said.

Ruby took a seat near the center. Pastor Meyers sat on her left, Gil on her right.

"As Pastor Meyers pointed out, I'm learning the ropes as bishop." She nodded to Gil. "Gil Ableman and I met with Pastor Meyers a couple of weeks ago. He told us what a great congregation you are."

She paused to let her words of praise sink in.

"Pastor Meyers tells us you are ready to call a pastor, despite the fact that you have five months or so to go on your term call. I am here to ask just one question." She looked at Gil, who smiled. "How can we help?"

Her question was met with initial silence.

Finally, Rosetta spoke up.

"Forgive us, Bishop Kinisa, but you've taken us by surprise. We are used to visitors from synod telling us what we should do. We are not prepared...."

Another council member interrupted. "The bishop asked a question, Rosetta. Let's not blow the opportunity. You know as well as any of us that we know the answer. We want a pastor. We've wanted one since Pastor Gottlund retired."

The floodgates opened. Andy started to talk about their ministry ideas that were dying while meeting after meeting was held about mission statements and "discernment." There was no denying how he felt by the way he spoke. He was tired and skeptical.

Andy continued. "Just because Pastor Gottlund retired doesn't mean we are lost in the wilderness. He was a good leader, but so are we. We really don't need months and months of interim work. I did some reading on this interim process. It's a ministry that is supposed to be at the request and call of the congregation. The synod forced this on us."

He turned to Pastor Meyers. "No offense, Pastor, but admit it. You have been following the directions of synod. We barely know NEWS from Adam and they don't know us from Eve. This is the first time the synod has talked directly to us in ages."

Ruby didn't comment. She didn't want to risk getting defensive and changing the focus of the meeting.

Each council member talked with passion about what they wished had happened during the previous year.

After a good airing, Ruby spoke again.

"I understand your frustration. It's time to move forward and I will make certain NEWS is there to support you in any way possible — even if it means staying out of your way."

The group felt the power in the room shifting — towards them.

Gil spoke. "Let's identify three congregational goals. We'll see if we can help."

"Goal One," Andy said. "We want to start the call process."

Rosetta chimed in. "Goal Two. We need to address the needs of families in the community. Our own families have been drifting."

An older man said, "Goal Three: Our people need to feel loved. We need an 'every member' visitation, so people know this is not just more of the interim process but that we are really 'back in business.'"

Ruby and Gil were impressed with the clarity.

Ruby summed things up, repeating the goals, and pledging NEWS support. "The search process begins today. Appoint a call committee, schedule a meeting with me next week, and I'll present some candidates."

Gil asked if there was anything else the group wanted to address. He was surprised when Ruby spoke up.

"I have a confession to make. This is not my first visit to Zion. I was here with you in worship a few weeks ago."

The group was shocked—Pastor Meyers most visibly.

"I have worked for NEWS for six years, but when I was elected bishop, I soon learned that I didn't know as much about all the churches as I thought I did. I knew the parishes I worked with as a staff member, but the others I knew only by reputation. Gil and I reviewed the parish records and I found the statistics to be alarming. I wanted to understand, but Gil advised me —wisely, I think — that my role as bishop would prevent people from sharing with me their true concerns."

Rosetta gasped. "You're Violet, aren't you!"

"I am Violet, and Violet is Bishop Ruby Kinisa. I apologize for the deception, but it has opened my eyes. I think I can now serve you better as bishop. I hope you understand. Thank you for your patience and forgiveness."

There was a pause as the council members took her words to heart. Council members looked from one to another. Pastor Meyers leaned back in his chair. Suddenly, Andy began applauding. The group joined him. One by one, they stood and offered their hands once again.

This time the handshakes were stronger.

14
Revelations

Ruby, Gil and Bruce met soon after the Bishop and Gil's visit to Zion Church in the city and Bishop Kinisa's revelation that she had visited in disguise.

"The cat's out of the bag now," Gil said. "Gossip travels fast in the church. You won't be able to stay under cover much longer."

"I suspect you are right," the bishop acknowledged. "If I am going to return to Pleasantville and Grace out in the country, I have to go very quickly. We did ask Zion's council to keep our visits secret, but I have a feeling there will be a leak."

Bruce laughed. "Yes, that technique never works—not even in the Bible. Jesus asked people to 'Tell no one.' We are still talking about his miracles today!"

"I feel sad that I may never again be able to use this tool," Ruby confessed. "I was learning so much! One of the challenges facing me will be to continue to learn about our churches without the subterfuge."

"It's too soon to measure the reaction of your Undercover Bishop visits, but judging from the standing ovation you got from Zion's council, there is hope that it will be successful across the board," Gil said.

"Your ploy is bound to generate a lot of buzz. If it's positive—and it seems like it could be—it could change some thinking. If we learn from this we may never have to use undercover techniques again. It's time to concentrate on building respectful relationships with our parishes."

Ruby could see that Gil was feeling relief. She had worked with him for six years but had never noticed how concerned he was. She was beginning to see a new Gil — and one for whom she had increasing respect.

"On Saturday, I'll go to the Women's meeting at Grace. Sorry, Bruce, but this one has to be solo. You won't fit in!"

Gil and Bruce both laughed.

"Meanwhile, let's schedule a meeting with Pleasantville's leaders."

Gil suddenly looked concerned.

"What is it, Gil?" Ruby asked.

"Just be careful. Pleasantville has been burned over and over by 'meetings with the synod.' Thy are likely to refuse and become defensive."

"Well, then how can I lead them?"

"It's going to be tough. We have to rebuild trust. After years of being ignored, they will see any initiative coming from synod as an attempt to take control. This is where your Undercover Bishop exercise will have its greatest challenge."

Gil took a deep breath, paused for a moment, and continued.

"You ask 'How can I lead them?' The answer is you may not be able to lead them. When you reveal yourself to Pleasantville, don't expect to be welcomed as you were at Zion. You may have to think in terms of serving them, not leading them.

"In Pleasantville, you will have to begin by accepting them as they are. They have survived more in their history than most churches. They have good instincts and good lay leaders that deserve credit. Frankly, the people of Pleasantville are going to trust their local leaders before they trust you. Really, that's the way it is in all churches. It's just exaggerated in Pleasantville because of the long history of poor relationships with your predecessors. They know their leaders. You are a stranger — a stranger who started her relationship with them by deceiving them."

"I think I understand," Ruby admitted. "But it makes me incredibly sad."

"I've been sad for a long time," Gil confessed. "For the first time, I'm feeling there may be some hope for some of the congregations we have been ignoring."

"Gil, how did things ever get this bad!"

"Ruby, I could write a book on that! There were economic forces as well as philosophical shifts that were leaving the small congregations behind. Societal changes were happening faster than ever before. Suburbia was a new thing and it was attractive to lots of people and lots of pastors. Affluence was becoming a mark of ministerial success."

Bruce spoke up for the first time. "I've been in seminary for nearly four years. I can tell you what I heard about small churches. 'Stay away' is the advice. If it is not coming from the professors, it's part of the student grapevine."

Bruce continued. "I'm really glad for the opportunity to travel with you incognito, Bishop Kinisa. I saw things I never learned in seminary. It has definitely changed my perspective! Now I understand the experience of one of my classmates. She was so tired of hearing gossip about one of the nearby congregations that she decided to visit them one Sunday morning. She came back impressed and the next time the subject came up, she set us straight."

"Undercover Seminarian?" Gil quipped. Bruce laughed.

"Bruce, would you consider a call to a small church?" Bishop Kinisa asked.

"I'd have to think about it and explore the economics, but yes I could see myself serving in the small neighborhood setting."

"When this is over, let's talk, Bruce. Maybe we can find a way to make ministry work for both the pastors and the congregations."

15
Grace in the Country Revisited

The next Saturday, Bishop Ruby Kinisa prepared for her return to Grace, the little church on the fringe of the synod's territory. As she donned her disguise she wondered how many more times she would transform to Violet. She laughed at the thought. Violet was taking on a personality of her own! "Definitely time to end the charade," Ruby thought as she completed her transformation.

She drove for an hour through the beautiful countryside, unconsciously noting each Lutheran church she passed and trying to picture the pastor serving it.

When she finally reached Grace, she entered the small church through the same doors that led to the sanctuary. This time she walked straight ahead ignoring the steep sanctuary steps by the entrance. She entered a fellowship hall abuzz with the chatter of women. Most of the ladies were seated at a long table, piled high with batting and cloth remnants. A sewing machine had been pulled into the center of the room. One woman was guiding some cloth under its needle. Some of the ladies had scissors and measuring tapes in hand. Others were threading needles for hand sewing. They all looked up. One of the ladies recognized her from her worship visit.

"Welcome back, it's Violet, isn't it?"

"Yes, I'm Violet," she answered, "and thank you. I thought I'd check out your women's group."

"Why, you are most welcome. I'm Ruth."

"I remember you, Ruth," Violet said. "We had a cup of soup together."

Ruth took a moment to introduce each lady. Each looked up from her work with a smile. Ruth explained,

"We are making cancer dressings for the local nursing home. Would you like to help?"

"I'm not sure I'll be of any help," Violet answered. "I've never been much of a seamstress."

One of the ladies called out, "Don't let that stop you. Pull up a chair. We'll find something for you to do."

Violet was interested and began asking questions. Her first questions were about the project, but she found the group of ladies to be so congenial that she soon felt comfortable asking all kinds of questions.

She learned that the group met every other Saturday, alternating between a service project and Bible Study.

The ladies asked questions, too. They wanted to know how she had happened to visit them, what brought her to Center Township, her family, her church background.... "Their curiosity is insatiable," Violet thought. She actively tried to bring the attention back to Grace and away from her.

Violet began asking questions about the men, youth, and children. The women didn't mind answering.

They went on to explain their approach to ministry.

"If the people of Grace see a need, they will find a way to answer it," Ruth explained. "It's not really organized."

"Ruth, you make it sound like we are disorganized," one woman complained good-naturedly. Everyone laughed heartily. Violet sensed there was an inside joke.

Violet decided to be quiet and do some listening. Slowly, the conversation drifted to the interests of the ladies.

"What are we going to do with all the children who are coming to church by themselves," one lady asked. "Does anyone have any ideas?"

"Maybe we should try to contact the parents and invite them."

"They won't come," another said. "We are free babysitters." Several grumbled in agreement.

"Maybe so," Ruth said. "But that gives us an opportunity. What if this is God's way of directing our ministry...of showing us the way."

No one objected. The ladies worked in silence for a bit.

"Let's stop what we are doing and pray for these children, right now." Ruth said.

Violet was surprised that there was no hesitation. Scissors, needles and thread, and measuring tapes were all placed on the table as heads were bowed. Ruth led the prayer.

Father, we turn to you today with concern for the children
you have brought to our door....

The impromptu prayer lasted for several minutes. Ruth's words had a way of defining the issue before them.

When the prayer ended, work resumed. After a few minutes, one of the ladies offered. "Let's each of us 'adopt' one of the children. We can each pray for one specific child."

"They'll never agree."

"They don't have to know that we are praying for them. After church, we can go out of our way to greet our 'adopted' child."

"Sounds like something we could do," one said.

"It might be a good start," another added.

"We'll be undercover prayer warriors," one of the younger women quipped. They all laughed and added to the analogy.

Violet choked, remembering her own "undercover" status.

Violet found the process she was witnessing to be fascinating. "We talk about holding visioning meetings and discernment sessions to help congregations determine ministry direction. They are doing this all on their own!" she thought.

Violet helped measure and cut fabric for about two hours and then excused herself. The ladies of Grace thanked her for her visit but explained that their meeting would go on for another hour or so. They invited her to return in two weeks for their Bible study.

As Violet retraced her route home, she once again took notice of each Lutheran church she passed. This time she wondered how many of them were planning their ministries like Grace.

16
Pleasantville Revisited

Bishop Ruby Kinisa was not looking forward to returning to Pleasantville. This small town, neighborhood church had all but split from the NEWS Lutheran Synod. She greatly respected the ministry effort she had witnessed during her two visits, one to a potluck fellowship dinner and one to worship. She was afraid that revealing herself as bishop would spark a protest and further set back Synod's relationship with the congregation. Besides, she liked the people she had met in Pleasantville. She didn't want to disappoint them.

Ruby, disguised as Violet one last time, arrived early for Sunday morning worship in Pleasantville. She had guessed that Bob and Martha Forster would arrive before everyone else, and she was right.

She found Bob folding the church bulletins and Martha setting the coffee urn to brew.

Both Martha and Bob were delighted to see Violet. They

greeted her warmly. Violet approached them more seriously than she had in the past.

"I wonder if I might treat the two of you to lunch after worship," Violet offered. "I'd really appreciate a chance to talk with you privately."

The unusual request surprised Bob and Martha. They looked at one another and came to a tacit agreement. "Sure, Violet, we'd love to join you, " Bob said.

Martha added, "Is everything all right, Violet?"

"I think so," Violet answered. "I just have some news I need to share with you."

Martha and Bob accepted the explanation and returned to their duties. Bob handed Violet one of the freshly folded bulletins. She entered the sanctuary and found a seat.

She sat for a few moments in the quiet sanctuary and then knelt in prayer.

Heavenly Father, be with me today as I talk with
Pleasantville's leaders. Forgive me if I was wrong to fool
them....

Violet prayed until at last she heard the electric piano sound the first chords of a medley of favorite hymns. Violet recognized one of her favorites. "Just as I am without one plea." As the pianist replayed the hymn in various interpretations, Violet repeated the words in her mind.

The service was beautiful just as it had been at her last visit. This time, Bob Forster gave the meditation.

Violet's concern for the luncheon meeting she had just arranged preoccupied her thoughts. Much of the meaning of the service passed her by.

After worship, several of the Pleasantville members greeted her. They were beginning to recognize her.

The more pleasant they were, the guiltier Violet felt. She was relieved when the last congregant left and Bob and Martha locked the door.

"I'm in your territory," Violet said. "I hope you can suggest a place that offers great food and is quiet enough that we can have a good talk."

"I know just the place," Martha said, "and it's just a short walk from here."

The three walked along the sidewalk of the main street of Pleasantville to a small family restaurant. Bob greeted the host and asked for one of the corner booths.

They settled in and ordered coffee. When three mugs were delivered to the table, Violet knew the time she had been dreading had come.

"Bob and Martha, I have a confession."

Bob and Martha set their mugs on the table and turned their full attention to Violet.

"I recently found myself facing a very difficult job. When I accepted the position, I thought I knew everything there was to know about the work. I was full of ideas I wanted to put to use right away. As I set to work, I soon realized I have a lot to learn."

Neither Bob nor Martha looked away. The conversation was taking a mysterious turn but their concern was for Violet. Violet noticed and felt all the more guilty.

"Bob, Martha," she started. "My name is not Violet. I am Ruby— Ruby Kinisa, the newly elected bishop of NEWS Synod of the National Lutheran Church."

Bob and Martha leaned back. Neither said a word. The expressions on their faces were flat. Ruby could read neither surprise nor anger. She continued her story.

"I started my position just a few weeks ago and reviewed all the parish records. I found some things that were troubling. Questions were jumping out at me from those printed reports. Why is attendance down? Why is support shrinking? Why are educational offerings dying? Why do so many churches have minimal pastoral services? I looked for answers, but I was advised by someone on the staff with more experience than I that I should try to find the answers myself."

Bob interrupted. He tapped his fingers on the table. "Can I guess? Pastor Ableman?"

"Yes, Gil Ableman advised me that appearing as bishop would stop people from sharing their concerns with candor. He told me people tell the bishop what they think the bishop wants to hear. He warned this applies to clergy as well as laity. He said I need to find a way to learn about the congregations and their challenges firsthand."

"Good man—Gil," Bob said.

Martha at last broke her silence. "So what have you learned, Vio-, I mean Bishop Kinisa."

"I have learned not to rely solely on parish reports for information. I have also learned not to rely on clergy impressions. They have a vested interest in their analysis and in their relationship with me."

Bob and Martha took some time to digest Ruby's words. Both seemed annoyed—Bob more so than Martha. Ruby feared the worst was about to happen.

"So how about Pleasantville? What do you think of us?" Bob asked at last.

"Bob, Martha, you are both doing a wonderful job in Pleasantville. You have an active church with willing and able members. NEWS has neglected you for a very long time and your members have kept the faith and a sense of mission. I commend you."

"Is there a 'but' coming," Martha asked nervously.

"There is no 'but.'"

"Does NEWS have a plan for Pleasantville?" Bob asked. "If they did, it would be the 'flavor of the month.'"

Ruby registered his annoyance.

"Bob," Bishop Kinisa started, "let me assure you. I have no plan.

I'm starting by talking with you. At your pleasure, I'll be glad to meet with your full council or even the full congregation. When I meet with your leaders or the congregation, there will be just one question on the floor: How can I, as bishop of NEWS Synod, be of service to the Christian community in Pleasantville?"

"Are you sure?" Bob asked. "No pastors you are trying to unload on us? No mergers with other congregations? No threat of closure?"

"Just the one question," Bishop Kinisa stressed. "We'll find the answers together."

Bob and Martha lifted their mugs of steaming coffee to their lips slowly and in unison. They each took a sip and replaced their mugs on the table.

They leaned back and thought for a moment, looking occasionally into Ruby's eyes and then to one another. Ruby felt her face turning red.

Finally, Bob spoke.

"Bishop Kinisa, welcome to Pleasantville. We have a council meeting scheduled for Friday night. We'd be very happy to have you as our guest."

Ruby breathed a sigh of relief.

The waiter came and took their order for Sunday brunch. The three chatted with energy all through salad, soup, lunch and dessert. Bob and Martha gave them an advance rendition of what they thought the rest of the church council would like to discuss.

As they walked back to the church parking lot, Bishop Ruby Kinisa apologized profusely. Bob and Martha accepted graciously.

"See you Friday," Martha called out as Ruby pulled away.

TOPICS and QUESTIONS for DISCUSSION

How would you define Church community?

How large must a church be to qualify as Christian community?

How can small churches meet the same economic demands of larger churches?

What do the three churches (city, small town and country) have in common? How do they differ?

You might make a chart with the names of each church, pastors and key members to help you remember. Ask your members to supply the information by way of review.

Pleasantville	Zion	Grace
Small Town	Urban Neighborhood	Rural on the Edge of Suburbia
No Pastor	Interim Pastor Pat Meyers	Pastor John Mintner
Carla, Earl Bob and Martha Forster	Rosetta Gorton Andy	Alex Ruth

Can your congregation identify with Pleasantville, Zion and Grace? Tell your story.

Is it better to have no church than to have a small church without a pastor?

How do you think the discussions with the congregations went when Bishop Kinisa returned and revealed her undercover status? Role play how those discussions might have gone.

At the end of the TV series, *Undercover Boss,* the CEO reveals his or her identity and rewards the employees who exceeded company expectations. Sometimes the rewards benefit others. Sometimes they directly influence the life or career path of the individual. How might Bishop Kinisa "reward" the members she encountered?

Statistically most people belong to small churches. Why do some people choose to belong to a small church? Why do others prefer larger churches? What benefits do small churches offer that larger churches are unlikely to meet? How can each serve the greater Church?

What do small congregations expect from their regional body? What do regional bodies expect from small congregations? How are these united or in conflict with mission?

Why is it that small churches could survive (and in fact were the norm) when our nation was much less affluent?

Pleasantville revealed that they hadn't been able to start a website with their previous pastor, but the youth tackled the project after the pastor left. How do congregations introduce innovative ministries that might not be within the pastor's skill set or interests? How can small congregations find the skills they need that might not match their pastor's skills?

Carla comments that Pleasantville Church would not know what they would do without Bob Forster. How do small churches nurture new lay leaders for the future?

How can a small church with limited funding take steps toward growth?

What are roadblocks that keep congregations from working together either within their denomination or with other neighborhood churches?

Is teamwork more likely with or without pastors involved?

Discuss the following quote from a popular book used by several denominations to train regional church leaders.

> "You do not have the luxury of giving everyone who asks for help whatever time you have available. Some tough decisions need to be made as to where your Regional Body is going to invest time, energy, and resources. Thinking in terms of TRIAGE is a most responsible thing to do at the present time. Congregations that will die within the next ten years should receive the least amount of time and attention. They should receive time that assists them to die with celebration and dignity. Offer these congregations a 'caretaker' pastor who would give them quality palliative care until they decide to close their doors. It is the kind of tough-minded leadership that will be needed at the helm if your organization is to become a Transformational Regional Body."
> —Transforming Regional Bodies,
> co-authored by Roy Oswald and Claire Burkat (2001)

Is ten years of palliative care a good investment of church funds and talents? Could ten years be better spent? How?

Should congregations be informed that their pastor is there to help them die? Should caretaker pastors get full pay?

What alternatives are small congregations hoping for?

Is an investment in a pastor the best use of congregational resources? What for example might happen if a congregation that was five years into palliative care and anticipating closing, was suddenly the recipient of a large endowment? How might this change relationships and ministry?

What role should pastors play in small churches where funding limits their time? Is there a way to reallocate church roles so that pastoral skills can be put to use where they are most needed?

List priorities that might move a congregation in the direction of growth rather than marking time?

Does the popular adage "go big or go home" apply to churches?

From the outset, Bishop Kinisa chose to attend more than the congregation's Sunday worship. How would her experience have differed had she attended only worship?

Discuss the role of lay leaders in your church? Are there problems? Do things run smoothly? What training would your lay leaders appreciate? How can small churches acquire the skills required to grow a church?

Imagine you are a visitor to your congregation. Describe your experience.

What would you expect of an interim ministry? Has an interim period helped or hurt your congregation? How so?

Imagine you are part of a congregation that is aging. How can Christian community serve the aging AND take steps to rejuvenate your congregation?

How familiar are you with nearby ministries in your denomination or congregations belonging to other denominations? How might knowing more about them influence your congregation?

What would happen to your members if a decision were made to close your church? How would this action impact the community?

In chapter 14, Gil lists some factors that influence downward trends in the church as we have known it.

> "Ruby, I could write a book on that! There were economic forces as well as philosophical shifts that were leaving the small congregations behind. Societal changes were happening faster than ever before. Suburbia was a new thing and it was attractive to lots of people and lots of pastors. Affluence was becoming a mark of ministerial success."

Discuss his ideas and add your own thoughts and experiences.

Most congregations fit into the two smallest categories of "church.." What is the value of a small congregation? Why do people join small congregations? How does a small congregation maintain its value as a small church within the church and still compete for services within the church.

If the entry point for church activity is usually the small church, and small churches are closed, how will larger churches meet the needs of all the neighborhoods left with no church presence?

The Redeemer Ambassadors

Members of Redeemer Lutheran Church, in the East Falls neighborhood, in Philadelphia, Pa., were evicted from their property by the Southeastern Pennsylvania Synod (SEPA) of the Evangelical Lutheran Church in America in September 2009, following litigation involving a property dispute and the interpretation of Lutheran constitutions. Courts ruled, without hearing the case, citing no jurisdiction in church matters. Redeemer was ordered to turn its property over to SEPA Synod—despite the ELCA's promises forbidding this. The Pennsylvania Appellate Court supported the ruling in a split en banc decision (5-2). The two dissenting judges wrote that *if the law were applied,* Redeemer's position has merit and the case deserved a hearing.

Litigation, against individual lay members, continued for several more years.

The gift of a large endowment at a time when SEPA Synod was intent on closing the church sparked the long-standing problems between Redeemer and SEPA.

Today (2014), nearly five years after the eviction, the church doors remain locked. The coveted building is unused.

Redeemer members continue to work and worship together. We visit the congregations that supported the taking of our property. We worship in our own neighborhood in borrowed space once a month. We pioneer online ministry.

Redeemer's Ambassador visits reveal common problems and the general lack of solutions available to congregations. Almost all congregations, large and small, are in statistical decline, some dramatically so.

Our visits reveal some troubling practices and attitudes. They also reveal that the church is running on the passion of a largely unrecognized laity.

*There is more mission potential in an open church
than in a closed church.*

*There is more economic potential in an open church
than in a closed church.*

For resources and ministry ideas for small churches, please visit

2x2virtualchurch.com

2x2virtualchurch.com provides laity a platform for their unfiltered voice on topics and church practices which directly impact their faith and their communities. Join the discussion!

Our primary interest is empowering the laity, but clergy are welcome, too!

Online courses include:

Developing Mission Statements
Branding for Evangelism
Fostering A Welcoming Environment for Worship
Developing A Congregational Social Media Strategy
Forming A Social Media Task Force
Teaching in Worship

Regular Blog Offerings include:
Object Lessons to Engage the Entire Congregation in Learning (more than 100 on file)
Slideshows to Use in Worship
Editorial Calendars for Online Ministry

These topics get weekly attention and are indexed for long-term use.

www.ingramcontent.com/pod-product-compliance
Lightning Source LLC
Chambersburg PA
CBHW070204060426
42445CB00032B/1213